SOMEONE TO WATCH OVER ME

An essential guide to godparenting

PICTURE E NJAU

BY

Peter Hinton and Iona Joy

With cartoons by Sarah O Hinton

Published 2006 by arima publishing

www.arimapublishing.com

ISBN 1 84549 076 2

Printed and bound in the United Kingdom

Typeset in Verdana 11/14

arima publishing

ASK House, Northgate Avenue

Bury St Edmunds, Suffolk IP32 6BB

t: (+44) 01284 700321

www.arimapublishing.com

Foreword

In African churches throughout the continent we offer the prayer:

God bless Africa
Guard her children
Guide her leaders
And give her peace

It is in the area of guarding her children that this book is speaking.
We rightly see children as a gift from God and also that they are our future. How they are reared and how they develop will not only determine their future but also the world of tomorrow.
All over the world children need good role models and valuable input from the adults in their community. In urban settings and with extended families separated by miles, the need for a community concerned for the well-being and growth of children is vital. Such a need is aggravated where HIV / AIDS and the break up of marriages leave so many single parents or orphans. It is into such a need that godparents can step and play their part in nurturing the child. Godparents form part of the community looking to guard the child and help him or her realise their full potential. This book provides practical ways to assist parents in choosing the godparents for their children – people who can play a vital role in the child's growth. It also provides guidance and ideas to help godparents perform the role in a very busy world where the building of relationships is ever important
I often encourage young people to reach for the stars. I hope this book will encourage parents and godparents to help children do just that.

Desmond Tutu
Archbishop Emeritus
Cape Town
South Africa

Acknowledgements

We would like to express deepest thanks to those who answered the godparenting questionnaire and provided the stories from their own experiences highlighted in the boxes throughout the book.

Special thanks to those who read the script and provided invaluable feedback - particularly L Owen, C Manuel, S Hinton (nee Colburn), A Duce and J Cooke. Also to Christian who edited the first draft of this book.

And to Alan Gordon Walker who guided us on our way.

The authors would also like to acknowledge the following for permission to reproduce copyright material. The authors would be interested to hear from any copyright holders not here acknowledged:

Seren for Sometimes from Selected Poems by Sheenagh Pugh, published by Seren (1990)

Peter Hinton, Botswana
Iona Joy, London

January 2006

To our godparents and godchildren

CONTENTS

Chapter 1

THE NEED FOR GODPARENTS TODAY?

Introduction

When Richard was asked to be a godfather to Emma he felt flattered and honoured. When, however he reflected on the invitation and asked himself what exactly was expected of him he had to admit that he hadn't a clue.

The collective noun for godparents based on questionnaires and interviews conducted for this book appears to be "a guilt" of godparents. Ask any godparent how they are finding the experience, and the answer invariably is one of shortcoming. "I'm not a very good godfather." or more directly "I'm a useless godmother!" are common responses.

Far from wishing to increase the guilt factor this book looks to reduce it and shift the collective noun to a "gratitude" of godparents. Gratitude in four ways:

- Godparents feeling grateful for the privilege of being asked to play an important role in the upbringing of the godchild;
- Godparents being grateful for the enjoyment the relationship brings over time;
- Godchildren being grateful for the interest and love shown them by a godparent, and
- Godchildren being grateful for the relationship that develops.

The guilt felt by most godparents may be down to being unclear as to what is expected or involved. People feel privileged being asked, and register the importance, but feel they are somehow falling short of hazy expectations. A better job description would clarify godparent's objectives.

Taking the UK as an example, 25-30% of children born are christened. In 2001 this amounted to approximately 168,000 children.[1] If for every child christened there are three godparents, an average of 450,000 people become godparents every year. Added to this are the large number of godparents with godchildren in existence. Just taking godchildren below the age of 16 and using similar statistics to those above, it seems there must be over six million godparents in the UK alone with godchildren under the age of 16.

Being a godparent can be hugely rewarding and exciting, and need never be viewed as a chore or duty. This book looks to demystify the role and function of godparents, both secular and sacred, and attempts to clarify the values, responsibilities and attributes that can be reasonably expected of a godparent. Given that once undertaken it is difficult to resign from being a godparent, this book aims to

[1] National Statistics Office/Church House

help all godparents to be better, more resourceful, imaginative and realistic in their roles. The book also tries to show how the natural parents can help the godparents fulfill their roles and vice versa. We examine how and why the role is relevant today, and in the process hope to go some way to enable godparents and those who choose them to maximize the potential of the relationship.

Godparents for the 21st century

When society was less secular than it is today being a godparent was straightforward. Chapter 2 sets out the background and traditional role. Today that is not the case and the role of godparenting ranges from the spiritual to one where a sibling or best friend is almost given a loyalty award. The resulting obligation is that the godparent remembers - or forgets, as the case may be - birthdays and Christmases. We seek to update the various changes to the role of the godparent that have evolved, both the traditionally Christian ideal as well as the more secular.

Rites of passage are as important in the 21st century as they have been for millennia. The naming of a child and the related ceremony of giving thanks appears to be a key rite of passage in many countries. The provision of godparents to a child at such an event should mean that they will take an interest in and play a role in the child's future and the child's own rites of passage. Godparents can provide an important support to child and parents throughout the upbringing of the child.

Moreover, social trends in both the developed and developing worlds would encourage the conclusion that there is a greater need today for godparent figures than ever before. This is the case in the **developed** world when one considers:

(i) The decline of extended families

When extended families were effective social units godparents could be seen as a beneficial extra. With the decline of the extended family godparents can now be seen as much more of a necessity. The greater mobility of a workforce that frequently relocates because of work has also put pressure on family units and reduced the support network normally available. The presence of a significant adult interested in the godchild is thus doubly beneficial.

In Ireland, Gerry was the oldest child of the eldest brother in a family of 11. When numerous cousins were born, Gerry being the eldest cousin was dragooned in to being a godparent. Since this typically meant a day off school and a party he fulfilled his obligations with equanimity. How many godchildren he has godfathered and what their names are is a mystery – what was important was that the children concerned had a younger godparent who is a relative.

(ii) The break up of marriages

The increasing break up of marriages leads to a situation where a child is likely to have fewer adults with influence in his/her life and fewer potential role models. With single parent families this gap has been most noticeable with teenage boys. A godfather can, to some extent, help fill the gap left if the natural father is no longer on the scene and provide a valuable role model.

(iii) Single parent families

Single parents bringing up children is a common occurance today through the death of one partner or through the deliberate choice normally of the mother to have a child but not the involvement of the child's natural father.

In the **developing** world urbanisation has resulted in a fall in the number of adults involved in the upbringing of most children. Historically, in Africa for example, village elders plus uncles and aunts would have been around to support the moral and character development of a child. However, many children today are brought up in cities by the mother or father, or often just the mother. In rural India children growing up in the village could be taken in by an artist, a mystic or other artisan who could teach them what they would need to learn. With the decline in traditional customs this role is disappearing. Consequently the support network that used to be around to assist with the upbringing of children has often disappeared. The impact of Aids is compounding the situation leaving many children without one or both parents.

In Uganda a child will have two godparents - one male and one female sibling of the parents. Non-relatives are not appointed. The responsibilities are to attend birthdays, marriages and other important events throughout the child's life. The godparents are to be a source of advice and guidance on any and every aspect of life. If one of the parents dies the godparents are to take an active involvement in raising the child - perhaps even taking the child into one of their own homes. In the tragic event of both parents dying the godparents use any legacy to bring up the godchild.

With the decline of the support network necessary to bring up children throughout the developed and developing world, godparents can play an increasingly vital role. In effect they become part of the virtual extended family- committed to supporting the parent(s) in the role and being involved with the child as it grows up. Providing this stability, even where large distances separate, may prove invaluable, particularly if there is a death or the parents' marriage ends. In such circumstances, supporting the remaining parent can become an important part of the godparent's role.

Both in developed and developing countries a set of loyal, conscientious and active godparents has never been more important than it is today. In a world where families are seldom surrounded by close family and friends, godparents can provide a means of support to parents in their role as primary rearers as well as being part of the child's social infrastructure. Through being a "significant adult other" in a child's life, and by becoming a trusted friend of the godchild, the godparent can play an important part in the child's growth and maturity. Well-chosen godparents will serve to improve the life of any godchild in many ways, as well as providing a number of role models, guides and points of reference for the child in question.

Other religions

Godparenting has grown out of the Christian faith and is often practiced in societies where there is a catholic or protestant tradition. Other religions do not appear to have godparenting or a similar practice. However, in many of the societies where, say, Judaism, Islam, Buddhism and Hinduism would be practiced there are strong extended family networks contributing to the nurture (spiritual, emotional and educational) of children. If all children would benefit from godparents then these major religions may wish to consider incorporating godparents for the children born into these faiths.

Godparents for everyone

Updating the role of the godparent for the 21st century requires adopting an approach that is both sacred and secular. Notwithstanding cultural or religious differences this book asserts that everyone should have godparents. Having significant non-family adults in a child's life should enrich the child's upbringing, broaden the role models he or she has to choose from, provide a mentor and guide throughout life and bring a source of emotional stability. Being accepted for who you are is one of the greatest gifts a child can receive. Godparents who can give such affirmation are giving something of inestimable worth.

Godparents or guideparents?

Some would argue that the term godparent is outdated and should be changed to say guideparent. Whilst there may be good reasons to do this it is unlikely that the fairy tale books will be re-written to replace fairy godmothers with an up to date term.

Godparents have been around for over two thousand years. Most people have one, some may be one or may have been asked to be one. Many countries have the practice of appointing godparents or their equivalent - a significant adult other with some form of spiritual responsibility towards the child concerned. In the same vein this book does not intend to change the terminology of centuries but rather investigate and update the role for today.

Chapter 2

A BRIEF HISTORY OF GODPARENTING, THE TRADITIONAL SERVICE AND ALTERNATIVE CEREMONIES

Where do godparents come from?

With no disrespect intended to the brothers Grimm, godparents did not originate in the land of wicked sisters and fairytales. How the fairy godmother came into existence is quite a mystery. The benign, kind-hearted, wand-waving figure coming to the rescue of maidens in distress does to a degree demonstrate certain positive godparent attributes - concern, kindness and timely intervention.

Why there were no politically correct fairy godfathers is also a puzzle. The nearest in the realm of books and film is the Mafia godfather figure. Caring for his own and defending those belonging to him are some of the better traits that could be emulated.

The true origins of godparents lie elsewhere.

Godparenting grew out of the Christian tradition of believers' baptism practiced by the early church. Baptism was originally introduced by John the Baptist to demonstrate people's repentance for the forgiveness of their sins. John stood in the river Jordan and baptized by immersing the entire person in the water. Christ, having been baptised by John, took up from where John left off and instructed his followers to go forth into the entire world preaching and baptising.

After Christ's death baptism became the initiation ceremony for those who having heard about Christ's life and teaching had decided to follow him and join the other followers of Christ. Here baptism signified repentance from sin and a turning to Christ as the divine son of God whose teaching and self-giving example new believers had decided to follow. In the early church baptism became the ritual of initiation of new converts into the Christian community. This was typically carried out in a river, pool or domestic bath house.

Although there appear to be cases in the early Church of whole families being baptized on converting to Christianity (e.g the New Testament accounts of Paul's jailer, Cornelius and Peter) child baptism seems to be the exception. Certainly as Christianity spread throughout the Roman Empire most early believers were adults and formerly followers of Judaism or other faiths. In the first century of the early church, Christians were persecuted and it was gradually felt that there was a need for a form of assurance that a person's conversion was genuine. This was primarily a means of protection against informers handing over names of Christians who would then be imprisoned, killed or become lion bate under Nero. Within this context the practice of appointing godparents, or sponsors, as they were known, developed. The sponsor to a recent convert wanting to be baptized would vouch for the person concerned and undertake to support the convert in becoming a faithful member of the Christian community.

In the fourth century after the conversion of Constantine to Christianity the rigorous scrutiny of the motives of people wishing to be baptized declined. However, over time the question arose of what should happen to children of believing parents. Should they be baptized while young, or should they wait until they could make the decision for themselves? The practice developed for children to be baptized, particularly given the desire that they should not die unbaptised. Gradually there was a transition from mainly adult baptism to almost exclusively infant baptism. The initiation ceremony that developed admitted children into the church using the process intended for adults but treating the child as an adult unable to speak. Thus developed the practice of godparents or sponsors answering on behalf of the child being baptized. Sponsors became known as the patron or "*patronus*." The *patronus* would undertake to protect the interests of the child and bring them up in the Christian faith. Natural parents originally took on this role until the ninth century, when godparents were expected to be adults other than the genetic parents. Even today in the Catholic Church godparents are not allowed to marry godchildren on the assumption that this would constitute intermarriage.

During the middle ages the Christian church in both East and Western Europe carried out the right of passage known as child baptism or Christening. With the age of discovery, the practice was exported to the New World by the Catholic church initially and protestant denominations later.

By the beginning of the 20th century child baptism was firmly established as a rite of passage practiced by many families throughout the world. Godparents would be chosen to share the responsibility of bringing the child up in the faith. The principle responsibility of the godparents - there were typically two, three or sometimes four - would be to encourage and bring the child up as a Christian. If the starting line was baptism then the finishing line for some Anglicans was confirmation and for Catholics was first communion. In confirmation the child, now probably a teenager, publicly confirmed the promises that had been made on their behalf by the godparents at baptism. The confirmation service included the making of the promises at baptism – namely-renunciation, affirmation of faith and promise of lifelong obedience to Christ.

For many godparents however confirmation is not seen as the green light to relinquish godparent responsibilities. The relationship and concern continue.

Godmother Agnes is typical saying, "I keep them forever, not just till confirmation."

The baptism service and alternative ceremonies

Given that godparenting developed within the Christian faith it is no surprise that most people take on godparenting responsibilities at baptism services in a church. This ceremony is where children become godchildren and consenting adults go from friend / relative to join the august body of godparents.

Set out below is a description of the typical baptism service, the promises made and an explanation of some of the symbolism and meaning. We then consider alternative services for use by those uncomfortable with the traditional service and lastly propose a ceremony for those wanting a secular format.

The traditional baptism service

The main features of the baptism service are:

1 Introduction

(i) Presentation

The child is presented for baptism by the parents (or in some traditions the godparents)

In Greece the godmother typically has the responsibility to choose the child's name. It has been known that a name such as Hypocrates is chosen which is of particular importance to the godmother but with no consultation with the parents.

(ii) The duties of parents and godparents

Typically the priest will say:
"Parents and godparents, the children whom you have brought for baptism depend chiefly on you for the help and encouragement they need. Are you willing to give it to them by your prayers, by your example and by your teaching?"
To which they reply, "I am willing."

Talking with God (praying) about the godchild, setting a good example by living in a way that is a positive role model and becoming a resource to answer questions as the godchild goes through life are all aspects of the traditional godparenting role.

(iii)The significance of baptism

The priest explains the symbolism of baptism whereby the child joins the community of Christians worldwide.

Since the story of the exodus of the Israelites from Egypt passing from slavery to freedom through the crossing of the Red Sea, water has had strong symbolism in the Christian faith. For Christians baptism symbolically represents the cleansing and forgiveness of sins and freedom from slavery to sin.

2 The Decision

This section comprises two sets of three questions reflecting the ancient act of renunciation and adherence to Christ practiced by the Eastern Church.

The priest addresses the parents and godparents saying. "I ask these questions which you must answer for yourselves and this child."

(i) First 3 questions

"Do you turn to Christ?"
"I turn to Christ."
"Do you repent of your sins?"
"I repent of my sins."

Repentance of sins is continual for any Christian. By dint of being human Christians do the things they shouldn't do and don't do the things they should. Forgiveness is obtained through repentance.

"Do you renounce evil?"
"I renounce evil."

A definite affirmation of the intent to not entertain evil and reject dishonesty, cruelty, selfishness and other destructive elements.

(ii) Second 3 questions

The priest addresses the parents and godparents on behalf of themselves and the child and asks:
"Do you believe and trust in God the father who made the world?"
"I believe and trust in him."
"Do you believe and trust in his son Jesus Christ who redeemed mankind?"
"I believe and trust in him."
"Do you believe and trust in his holy spirit who gives life to the people of God?"
"I believe and trust in him."

These central tenets of the Christian faith are affirmed.

In this section of the service the child's parents and godparents are, on behalf of the child, committing to live life in a relationship with Christ to whom the child being baptized now belongs.

3 Signing with the cross (chrismated)

The priest signs the child with the sign of the cross on the brow.

Sometimes performed with oil this historic act symbolises the child now belonging to God and that she shouldn't be ashamed of being known as a follower of Him. It also indicates that as a Christ follower the child has entered the challenge of taking up the cross, following him in the world and embarked on the way of love despite its costs.

Ambrose in 400 AD commented that the candidate was "anointed as Christ's athlete; as about to wrestle in the fight of this world."

4 Gift of water and baptism

The priest performs the ancient rite and bapitises the child saying, "..name of the child...I baptise you in the name of God the Father, Son and Holy Spirit."

The baptism marks the beginning of a new life following Christ. From now on the child's belonging to Christ should characterise their life.

5 Giving of a lighted candle

The giving of a candle is a medieval custom practiced in the West.

Symbolically the lit candle visually demonstrates the passing from darkness to light and the child's journey just embarked upon to walk in the light of Christ's teaching and example. It is also a reminder that Christ described himself as the Light of the world and would draw all people to himself.

6 Congregation welcomes the child into the church

The local Christian community also plays an important role in supporting parents and godparents in the bringing up of the child.

Alternative ceremonies

Is it not the case, however, that a significant number of parents and godparents who go through the traditional baptism service would not describe themselves as committed Christians? What place should faith play in performing their role of godparent? Should only committed Christians play that role? We argue that the role should be open to all but what are godparents to do in so far as it relates to the child's own spiritual awareness, development and thinking?

This issue of faith was discussed in The Times in a series of published letters in 2002. Questions and positions were raised including:

> *"Sir, I have been asked to be godfather to my best friend's daughter. I am not a regular churchgoer. Should I accept?"*

> *"Sir, I was an atheist when my brother asked me to be a godparent to his son. It was the highest compliment he could have paid me, and I would not have dreamt of declining."*

> *"Sir, Canon Saward (letter, May 24) accuses atheists who recite Christian phraseology at fonts of 'hypocrisy', a form of 'perjury', and 'smugly telling lies before God and others'."*

The above debate centers on the traditional definition and practice of godparenting within the church context. Chapter 3 of this book attempts to redefine the role from being a purely sacred one to something much wider. Within that definition a godparent of whatever religious persuasion can be concerned with the whole development of the godchild including how the child should be nurtured in the non-material realm of life. Having said that, we still need to address the issue of faith. Firstly, in how it relates to the ceremony itself and secondly (Chapter 8), in how a godparent can perform the role of encouraging the child's spiritual development if they are, say, a Christian, agnostic or atheist.

(i) Alternative church ceremonies

Many go through with the traditional baptism ceremony described above out of necessity because they think it the right thing to do or simply because there is no alternative means on offer of becoming a godparent. In the normal course of the standard baptism service, however, they would have been asked questions and make promises of Christian belief such as:

"Do you renounce the devil?"
"Do you accept Christ?" and
"Will you draw them by your example into the community of faith and walk with them in the way of Christ?"

Being asked in public such questions may have a solid historical background but for some is profoundly uncomfortable. If it is impossible to answer in the affirmative either nothing is said in reply, or an incoherent reply or grunt is mumbled. Introducing such discomfort and some would say "necessary hypocrisy", even dishonesty, in what should be a life affirming and joyful occasion raises questions about the suitability of the traditional baptism service today for significant numbers of people who can't answer those questions positively or with a clear, unambiguous conscience.

However, not withstanding the previous paragraph, the fact that so many people still go through with the traditional baptism service despite having issues with the declarations and promises they are asked to make would seem to underline the importance of marking the rite of passage of the gift of new life. If this rite of passage is to be celebrated would it not be better to have a ceremony that accommodates believers and non-believers alike? To address this issue we set out an alternative church service in Appendix 1. The alternative service proposed in Appendix 1 is for those who want a church service but without parents and godparents being asked to state things that they are uncomfortable with. Rather it looks to them to promise to contribute towards the child's development, to encourage the child to grow spiritually, emotionally and physically and, lastly, to be a guide and mentor. The alternative service has promises that committed Christians should be able to embrace as well as agnostics and atheists.

The use of this service will obviously have to be made with the co-operation and support of the priest concerned if held in a church.

(ii) Alternative secular ceremonies

For those who want a ceremony with no religious overtones, Appendix 2 provides another ceremony. This concentrates more on celebrating new life with parents and godparents promising to play their part in the child's growth and development. It is also the case that the increasing popularity of naming ceremonies indicates the attractiveness of other forms of celebrating the arrival of a child into the world.

Both the alternative church ceremony and secular ceremony proposed are designed to provide a format which parents and godparents can play with. As with marriage ceremonies and funerals, the more personal they are and the more shaped by the families involved, the more meaningful they tend to be.

Chapter 3

WHAT ARE GODPARENTS FOR?

The role today

Drawing on godparenting questionnaires and experience across more than 20 nationalities, the general consensus is that godparenting is valuable and should involve caring for the child, as well as some contribution to spiritual development.

Sybil, godmother of 15, says "I like Godparenting to have a Big G" – there are lots of other relationships: blood, patronage, sponsorship, or adoption to name a few- but all quite different from Godparenting. I like it that parents actually choose you and am keen on the religion related aspects.

Godparenting – a unique relationship

The focus in the godparent / godchild relationship is primarily on the godchild and his or her development. The godparent's role is to take a specific and direct interest in the growth and development of the child and to encourage the child's personal, emotional, physical, spiritual and cultural growth. At its best the godparent can become an independent and objective source of counsel, advice, friendship and mentoring. However, the godparent can normally only be effective in performing this role as their relationship with the godchild develops.

Where godparents are not related, blood ties do not create a familial obligation and the godparent performs his or her duties within the context of that unique godparent / godchild relationship. Here the interest shown and love given is purely voluntary and self-sacrificial.

Tim and Fiona gave birth to Joseph and asked their best man Philip to be a godparent. As a confirmed bachelor and business executive this provided Philip with the opportunity to be involved in the upbringing of a child – an experience he was unlikely to have himself. In the early years Philip bought presents and performed the traditional duty of holding baby Joseph as he threw up over his nice linen suits. Later they played football or cricket together and over time developed a special friendship. Philip would send postcards from his travels around the world – Nepal, Kyrgyzstan, Ouagadougou. Strange wooden elephants would arrive from Africa, Nasa space shuttle models from America, glass seals from Sweden.

In his teens Joseph began a cold war with his father and instead would confide in Philip about girls, drugs, his parents, A levels, gap year and choice of university. Tim and Fiona were grateful that their awkward teenage son had a safety valve in the form of Philip as guide and mentor. Joseph didn't always agree with Philip's views but respected and appreciated someone out of the family who he could talk to. Philip enjoyed the friendship that had developed and hoped he was providing a useful function.

The role in its fullest sense should consist of the following four key elements:

(i) Establishing a special relationship with the godchild

Being a godmother rather than an aunt or godfather rather than an uncle appears in practice to set the relationship apart.

Rebecca and Joshua share the same aunt. However, the aunt is also godmother to Rebecca. 5 year old Rebecca has been known to point out to younger brother Joshua that she had a prior claim to sit on her godmother's knee on account of being the goddaughter. Although her perceived rights are unlikely to stand up in a court of law it is clear that in Rebecca's eyes they are real.

This godparent / godchild relationship is distinct once it is created. There is nothing quite like it within the social fabric of many societies. The fact that for many it becomes dormant or non-existent is more a reflection of a lost opportunity than the pointlessness of it all. The significant number of godchildren who have benefited from a strong relationship with a godparent reveals how rich the relationship can be.

Melanie, a South African godchild, had a family friend as a godmother who took the role seriously. She would visit every couple of months specifically to see her godchild and have chats.

"The fact that she was not family was significant - she was out of the loop - an outsider, and I really listened to what she had to say."

Interestingly as the years have passed this godmother-godchild relationship has remained for Melanie. "My relationship with her is special ***because she is my godmother****."*

Part of nurturing the uniqueness in godchild Joseph's experience was that godfather Philip would produce presents just for him. While his siblings looked on in wonder their initial response of "Where's my present?" or "Why does Joseph get a present and not me?" over time subsided to be replaced by an acknowledgement that as Joseph's godparent, Philip had a special interest in Joseph.

Some godparents overcome with guilt or pity for the left out children end up buying presents for everyone.

Auntie Eileen used to do this for all four children at Christmas but only bought birthday presents for her godson James.

Andrew and Mary's 2-year-old daughter was so upset about being left out when her brother's godmother gave him gifts that the parents actually requested the godmother to refrain from giving until the child could cope.

Godparents shouldn't feel guilty over so deemed "preferential treatment" to godchildren over their siblings. Part of building up that relationship is underlining the special nature of it. In the early years, however, when siblings may find it difficult to understand why they have been left out, godparents may want to give Christmas presents (even token ones) to all the children.

Naturally, it is easier if all the children in a family have active godparents. In such circumstances each child will have their own special adult remembering them at certain times - hopefully bringing some equality to the situation and diffusing rivalry.

What is important here is that the godchild is important and special to someone - the godparent. Not because of blood relations or legal obligation but simply through having been invited and accepted. If all the child's godparents can communicate unconditional love a child will be in receipt of emotional scaffolding that will provide invaluable support throughout their life.

(ii) Providing a role model

Educationalists have long recognized the importance of role models in the healthy development of children. Recent research on teenage boys in the UK revealed that they actually need contact with a significant adult male, other than the father, if they are to mature properly. Similarly in cases where the godchild loses a parent through death or divorce, or was originally from a single parent family, the godparent of the same sex as the child can end up providing an important role model.

In the early years the godparent can become another parent figure but without the familial ties. As such he or she provides the child with a different model and someone to make comparisons with when looking at his own parents. This can vary from taste in clothing, cars, holidays, and jobs to interests and the way the godparent treats any partners. This latter aspect can become significant in the teen and early adult years when the godchild is forming his or her own views of what makes a relationship work. Since few marriages demonstrate a perfect role model, seeing how a godparent and partner interact can provide a valuable comparison out of which a "working model" can be created.

Andrew's natural father always used to say to him "You will learn from our mistakes!" This liberated Andrew from the expectation that his parents' relationship was perfect and free from criticism. When Andrew went to stay with his 2 godfathers for a week's holiday on separate occasions he saw how they operated at home. One was gentle and softly spoken – always treating his wife with respect and consideration. The other godfather was dynamic and very busy – seeming to leave the wife to take the strain of bringing up the 5 children. It wasn't much of a surprise that son number four was a tear-away and the youngest a brat. In his amateur attempts to make sense of life and relationships Andrew built up a model of what elements comprised a good marriage relationship – building on the good aspects from his natural parents, taking the good aspects from the other two, whilst at the same time making a mental note of some of the less than ideal components that were to be avoided if possible.

In many parts of rural Africa the village elders provide a role model for the young men. For centuries such a role has provided continuity and stability so that the next generation knew what was expected of it. Values were passed on as well as skills and traditions. Urbanisation has tended to undermine this practice and left a vacuum in the upbringing of the young. Could godparenting bring back some of the lost role modeling that used to take place in the villages?

(iii) Being a confidante, offering advice – back up and being there

Perhaps as important as being a role model is that of providing a listening service and offering impartial advice. If the relationship has developed and a suitable level of trust established then the godparent can be a source of guidance for the godchild at various stages and in a multitude of situations. This can be of real benefit at trying times of transition such as teens, leaving school, pre and post-university and when making career choices. The wealth of experience godparents have accumulated by dint of being alive can be invaluable in guiding a godchild as they make their own way through life.

When a godparent shares their own experiences of what they did when they met crossroads in their own lives this can be of immense assistance in helping a godchild think through their own situation. Prescribing a course of action is not the godparent's duty, rather, as with all good mentors, listening, sharing and helping the godchild make their own decision is the challenge.

John had been going out with Isabel for over 2 years when the two went to visit his godmother. After an enjoyable couple of hours the godmother addressed the unspoken issue, asking, "Where are you going in your relationship?" It was an explosive moment. It was one thing to ask a godson that kind of question in private but quite another to ask it in the presence of the female concerned! On the 200 mile journey home silence prevailed. On reaching the flat silence was followed by tears and sobs as the godchild and girlfriend agreed to have a break and compared diaries to decide who would cancel which social engagement. In the end neither could go through with the split and one year later John and Isobel were married. The godmother had expressed her concern that the relationship was drifting and asked a penetrating question. This acted as a catalyst and resulted in conversations that needed to take place and personal thinking and resolve hitherto lacking – particularly in the godson.

When the godparent / child relationship develops to its full potential the godparent can become a refuge and a confidante. Godparents can be pro-active in developing this aspect. Sometimes it can be for the protection of the child against self-destructive behaviour – particularly at times of inner crisis. For the godchild to know that the godparent will be there for them whatever happens is like taking out a gigantic emotional insurance policy.

In order to build the relationship and provide the basis for being a guide and confidante, a reasonable amount of effort will have been required to establish the requisite status and trust levels. A later chapter explores how this can be achieved through active contact.

A godparent can also back a godchild in some difficult decisions. Crisis periods are dealt with in more detail later, but at times parents may be too close to a situation to be supportive in a young adult's choice of action, and the godchild may need to draw upon a more impartial adult, their godparent, to support actions.

Natasha's father was an old friend of her godfather David's, but had left his wife for another woman. The turmoil of the divorce had led Natasha to re-examine her own values, and as a consequence she had decided (at the age of 17) to convert to Catholicism. Her father (a lapsed member of the Church of England) was furious and tried to block her decision. Natasha appealed to her godfather for advice and he was able to reassure her that if, in all conscience and after careful consideration of her motives it was her conviction to convert to Catholicism, then it was absolutely the right course of action. David's own faith was subsequently helpful as she struggled with the theology.

(iv) Mentor – the active responsibilities

A key element in godparenting is that of mentor.

A young offender recently underwent rehabilitation and vocational training at an excellent charity offering such support. He had had a miserable life. He was abandoned aged nine, was then in care, started truanting, was expelled from six schools, and was in and out of gang crime and youth offending institutions. By the time he was 18 he had been imprisoned four times, could hardly speak, lived on the street, and was unable to make eye contact with any other human being. He talked about how his life had developed this way, and he explained how demotivating his childhood and adolescence had been: no-one cared at home, at school class sizes were huge and he was categorised as a problem from the start; there was no adult "looking out for him". Had any of the schools provided him with a "mentor"? They hadn't. Would it have made any difference? His answer was surprising, as it was a resounding "yes". If just one adult had consistently taken an interest, praised him when he did right, listened to his side of the story when he was in trouble again, encouraged him in the few interests he had, then he would have seen the point of not "screwing up". He was very believable, because at the grand old age of 20, he was now a highly motivated car mechanic, able to articulate extremely perceptively the social problems of youth today. He was charming and humorous. And the reason for this transformation was clear: he was living in a community where he was respected and it included adults to whom he mattered.

Although it may be unlikely that anyone reading this book will have a godchild with such a colourful history, this illustrates how important the presence or absence of an influential adult or "mentor" is to a child whose world is uncertain and difficult. But the example bears out research which shows that one stable adult in a child's life can make a crucial difference.

In this role as mentor the godparent supports and encourages the child in their development in the following key areas:

Spiritual

Adopting a holistic approach to the godchild's development will involve encouraging the child to develop an understanding of the spiritual dimension of life and determine their own spiritual journey. As Plato said "*An unexamined life is not worth living*" (*Aplogohma).* Godparents have a responsibility to encourage their godchildren to examine themselves and reflect on the important things in life. Specifically in the 21st century where the prevailing culture is materialistic and individualistic the godparents have a key part to play in challenging the godchild to consider the great spiritual teachers the world has had and reflect on the relevance of their teaching to life today. The example of David and Natasha above is an excellent illustration of how a godparent with religious conviction can help a godchild in their own search for meaning.

By recommending spiritual classics and other books (see Chapter 6) the godparent can stimulate the child's thinking and spiritual development.

Temporal

When godparents look at the small bundle of godchildness on the day of the christening, the contribution that bundle will make to the world probably isn't the first thing that crosses their mind. However, reality will come to bear at some stage and making his or her way in life will need to be addressed.

Godparents can play a specific role in this through being confidante, guide and friend as explained above. In addition the godparent can act as a foil to any overbearing parent who may wish their offspring, for example, to make certain career choices. Helping the child to find a job, profession or activity it loves and can excel at is part of the godparent's role.

In Britain gap years between university and school or starting work have helped a wide variety of young people to have time to experience new cultures, jobs and activities, and provide time to think about the options. Godparents may be able to provide alternative ideas and even financial assistance to enable a godchild to take a gap year. In exploring different career options the godparent could use their networks to arrange for the godchild to talk to people operating in fields of interest to the godchild. When it comes to finding a job, again the godparents own contacts could be invaluable in at least getting an introduction or work experience.

Emotional

The emotional maturity of a godchild is difficult to gauge but the godparent has an advantage in being several steps removed from the daily interaction of parents with the child. Consequently, seeing the child intermittently can serve to leave an impression on how the godchild is growing emotionally.

Some godparents may want to help the godchild make use of personality-type systems of analysis. The Myers Briggs approach for example is based upon the personality typings known as Extrovert / Introvert, Intuitive / Sensing, Thinking / Feeling, and Judging / Perceiving. Having an outline understanding of this approach can help the godchild grow in his or her own awareness of their own personality type – with its own strengths and weaknesses.

When Ali's godmother discussed with her the Myers Briggs system the penny dropped that Ali responded to people and situations purely from a "feeling" basis. This had brought her into conflict with a number of boyfriends who had tended to be more "analytical" in their approach. Ejecting aforementioned men from her life on the grounds that they were unfeeling and hard-hearted she now started to realize that in some situations being a "thinker" was more appropriate than being a "feeler".

Educational

Godparents can play an educational role in the life of a godchild in helping the child to appreciate the world and the universe. In particular godparents can play an invaluable role in encouraging the godchild to explore and develop an interest in history, music, literature, theater, nature and all the multitude of other interests that can be enriching.

Chapter 6 provides gift and event ideas for godparents to draw on as they seek to support the godchild in its educational growth over the years. At the end of the day if the godparent has a passion for piston engines this is more likely to be contagious and interest the godchild than simply providing an encyclopedia on the subject. Such tomes can follow if an interest is ignited in the child.

Jemma's passion for vintage cars was borne from Saturday mornings passing spanners to her godfather repairing his 1920's Sunbeam. Now a godmother herself she takes her godson to vintage Silverstone and both enjoy the smell of burning oil as the ERAs hurtle round the bends.

When Paul decided to go to study theology in a gap year he undertook a variety of jobs to raise the necessary funding. Before he left his godmother kindly asked if he had sufficient and being slightly more realistic than Philip gave him a lump sum out of what she was planning to leave him in her will plus leant him an additional amount. Consequently Philip survived his year abroad and repaid the loan on taking up a job on his return.

For the entrepreneurial godchild a godparent with financial resources could even make an investment in a business venture. Any godparent making such an investment may be well advised to see such action as speculative and unlikely to result in a positive financial return.

Chapter 4.

WHO AND HOW DO WE CHOOSE?

Inviting godparents for your child

"I suppose we'd better ask Bryan to be Harry's godfather - I was his best man 3 years ago and he was always a laugh at Exeter and now that he's in the wine trade will presumably be good for a case of ----".

"But we haven't seen him since the wedding and what about my brother Mark? He asked me to godmother Milly and would be so upset if we passed him over."

"But they haven't got any money and even less taste. Which reminds me we owe the Outhwaites as I'm Freddie's godfather."

"But I'd prefer the Bletherington-Smythes as we could take Harry up to stay with them at Nobhill Park ".

If, as Billie Holliday said, "It takes a *baaadd* woman to be a good godmother", parents choosing godmothers had either better know some baaadd women or take out adverts in the small ads section of the local paper to find one.

More often than not, however, the process of selecting godparents is a complex process of disentangling a feudal web of which half of the couple has which obligation to whom, which potential godparent might have money to spare, and who can offer what. The interests of the godchild, the most important person in the triangle, of godchild, godparent and parent, are too often sidelined, yet it is ultimately his or her interests, and not those of the godparent or parent, which should be served.

The best way to serve a child's interests is to respect such feudal webs but not be constrained by them and to favour a creative approach. An examination of what influences are desirable for a child to come under is important. Did the parent lack particular input or encouragement in their own upbringing which now benefit their child? Did the parent benefit from a particular relationship which could be replicated in the child's life?

The ideal godparent won't necessarily be good with babies or toddlers, although if one is lucky they might take children off the parents' hands for a day, an evening or a weekend.

Godparenting is for life, not just until confirmation, and therefore it is worth bearing this in mind when deciding whom to invite.

How many godparents?

Traditionally in the UK girls have two godmothers and one godfather, boys two godfathers and one godmother. More recently two of each has become popular for both sexes, and as numbers of offspring dwindle and social circles widen some people are drafting in battalions of godparents. There is no hard and fast rule. A greater number of eggs in a variety of baskets increases spice and spreads risk, but may also devalue individual relationships. Knowing that you are one of six godparents to a child is not the same as being one of three.

Who owes what to whom?

The parents have to decide if they think someone would be right for their child, and there should be no obligation to "ask back". If parents are very happy with a relationship with a godchild and its parents, then reciprocation will reinforce an existing bond between families. The children may become "god-siblings" which could provide them with much enjoyment. However, it may be desirable to broaden horizons and consolidate relationships with other parties.

Anxiety about causing offence to the parents of an existing godchild can result in confusion. Probably the best way to avoid offence is to deal with it directly. Reminding the godchild's parents how much enjoyment is derived from godparenting *their* child and that as a consequence the friendship with them is very secure does little harm. However, they should be told that it has been decided to invite a third party for valid reasons; it is likely they will be understanding.

Blood relatives

This is a thorny issue. A set of godparents entirely consisting of the traditional uncles and aunts may short-change a child. The child will already have ties with this group of people, presumably including regular access and uninhibited affection, and the child's parents and their siblings should not need this additional connection to cement their sibling relationship. Uncles and aunts are "insiders" and in later life the child or young adult may want to look to an outsider for advice and guidance. Add to this the nightmare of selecting one sister over another and the endless possibilities of jealousy and offence and it can, simply put, be easier to look elsewhere. But sometimes uncles and aunts work well as godparents.

Twins Ellie and Sean have each claimed one of their mother's two sisters as a godmother. It has brought the relationships into greater focus which is helpful in an environment where the twins find themselves constantly lumped together as a single entity.

Generally speaking, though, uncles and aunts rarely disappear. The relationship is more likely to be "unconditional" –a crucial attribute to the godparent / godchild axis, and benefits from the longevity of acquaintance with the child's parent. Cousins or other relatives outside the immediate circle can confer similar but less claustrophobic benefits and help to cement relationships founded in childhood.

When, during Ryan's adolescence, his mother displays acute paranoia regarding the perils of drink, godfather Alex (his mother's cousin) will be well positioned to explain to Ryan that his late maternal grandfather was an alcoholic who regularly climbed onto the roof to threaten the worst and that consequently his mother is terrified that he will do the same.

A particular attachment to Aunt Agatha because she was the only one who would explain the joke about the duck and the drake to ten-year-old Lucy will render Aunt Agatha a pretty good godmother candidate for Lucy's daughter Kitty as well.

Age of godparents

It may be worth considering the age range of the godparent pool. Obvious candidates for the role will be friends of the parents and this generally implies that the godparent will be of a similar generation which may have its limitations. Looking to alternative generations may be inspired.

Robert has been Tom's professional and personal guru for many years, but is considerably older. Tom was considering Robert as a godfather to Paul, but was worried about Robert's age. Fortunately Robert has a wonderful teenage daughter, Daisy, whom Tom has known since babyhood. When invited, Daisy leapt at the role with more passion than the rest of the godparents put together and will no doubt provide an excellent bridge between Paul and his parents' generation when the trials of adolescence are under way. The glowing Robert meanwhile is spared such a commitment late in life and can derive enormous satisfaction from the endorsement of his own parenting skills.

The ancient and revered bring wisdom and serenity to many troubled episodes as well as additional years of experience and history beyond that of the parents. This may be an important consideration in cases where natural grandparents are not alive or around.

Which friends?

"New friends are silver but old friends are gold". So the saying goes and there is much truth in it. School and the years immediately following are often the period when really solid friendships are built. Enormous levels of trust and reliance can be built upon these foundations during the following years. These can provide ideal material for godparents - provided the relationships are still active and developing.

However, beware the college drinking companion known for 20 years but seen only once every three, when conversation is limited to the football results and reminiscing about the night spent in the can for being drunk and disorderly after painting the testicles of the college stallion fluorescent green. Bonding though this experience may have been at the time, check that there is more scope for growth in the relationship and avoid using the invitation to become a godparent as a sentimental attempt to rekindle something beyond its shelf life. This godparent may never be seen nor heard of again after the christening.

In reality however, friends that have endured the test of time will probably still be around for weddings and the next generation of christenings. Mixing friends from different phases of life is also a good idea as this will introduce people associated with the various aspects of the parents' lives.

Jack's parents met at university, and all his godparents were at university with his parents, which is excellent for the Jack Godparent Club but may mean that Jack won't meet anyone outside of this clique. Then when his little brother arrived, there were no university friends left for him and although he will benefit from a wide range of other friends, he will miss out on the university element of his parents' lives.

New friends are risky but also worthwhile.

When a colleague, known for under a year, asked Caroline to godmother her daughter, Caroline was initially quite taken aback. Granted, particularly given the eccentric nature of their working environment, there had been a pretty rapid meeting of minds, but so soon? Didn't they have other friends? (They did). Seven years later the godmother regards her goddaughter's family as her second home and recognises that the invitation, based on a gloriously optimistic vision of the future, has enabled a part of her life to flourish beyond expectation. No doubt this experience is equally rubbing off on her goddaughter.

Character

The most important factor in selection is that the godparent will be interested, not necessarily in nappy changing, but in the broad development of the child. The godparent should ideally have a demonstrable capacity for forming committed long-term friendships. A clue as to whether they have this capacity would be if they ever mention old friends and the extent to which they appear to treasure the relationships.

The godparent need not necessarily be "good", although a generous dose of benevolence is pretty essential.

Gerwyn once spent six months as a guest of Her Majesty but has since collected a handful of godchildren whose birthdays he forgets but to whom he is devoted. He will be extremely useful when Richard gets busted for drugs at school as Gerwyn will be able to explain, in detail, why getting on the wrong side of the law is a 'Bad Idea'. He will also be able to elucidate, clearly and succinctly, the difficulties of financing cocaine once it becomes habitual, and as Gerwyn is now a glamorous and widely published war correspondent based in Kabul, Richard is far more likely to listen to him than to his own father, who manages pension funds.

Rosie was quite nervous when Sally, a staunch Catholic, suggested she become Sophie's godmother. "Have you any idea what I got up to in my late teens and twenties?" "Shudder to think, but I shall be pointing Sophie in your direction for advice on men and sex."

A reformed cat-burglar or thrice-divorced man-eater may not be the perfect role model for your child, and these examples are extreme, but their sense of adventure and lively spirit may be characteristics you would want your child to emulate. And they do come with experience!

It would probably be wise however to mix a bit of "good" with the racy. If Richard's circumstances go badly wrong, and back up (temporary or permanent) is required, Gerwyn will be of little use in Kabul. In which case it will be fortunate that Polly, who bakes fabulous bread, goes to church most Sundays and keeps an open house, is on hand to steady the boat. Her humour and phlegmatic approach will be an invaluable haven amidst the turmoil of Richard's life.

Diversity

If one of the purposes of godparenting is to expose the child to the best and broadest experience life can offer, the selection process should follow this theme. A godparent array containing texture as well as solid sources of support and welfare will serve a child better than a monoculture of parent-clones. Godparents having complementary attributes will provide a more complete service and additionally the parents may benefit from fostering relationships with a diverse set of people rather than sticking to the usual crowd.

If one is fortunate, ones friends have a variety of talents and attributes. Not all of them (if any) will be wealthy, but they may have passionate interests, which will help to broaden a child's horizons. Assuming the godparents are within striking distance, the art historian can enliven a trip round the local gallery, a keen musician can introduce a child to the pleasures of ballet or jazz and most godparents can accompany the child to see a football match involving either the child or a professional team.

Steve, a travel-writer, will have his work cut out encouraging and advising no fewer than ten godchildren on expeditions before and during university, whilst George, a Texas-based horse trainer, cannot wait to get godson Jeff onto the back of a sensible mare.

Of course wealth is useful. However the man or woman with a key to an appreciation of adventure may, in the long run, be more beneficial to the child than a cash cow.

If one really wants to equip a child with the broadest possible outlook, then involving someone from a different background or culture is worth bearing in mind. If the godparent lives or is likely to live on another continent, then it will be necessary to trade the ability of the child to get to know its godparent through regular meetings for the exoticism of having a godparent in Nepal and the possibility of visiting them in due course. However, letters and emails can bridge the gap, and although the godparent will be seen more rarely, it will probably be for longer periods and bring a rich dimension to the life of the child.

Ed's parents worked in Fiji when he came to be baptized so two Fijians were asked to be godparents. Exotic as this was unfortunately when Ed and his parents left Fiji the contact dwindled and died. Should Ed decide to visit Fiji in the future, however, he feels he would be quite entitled to contact his wayward godparents and visit them.

Emma, an only child, would have been a bored and disaffected public school product, but fortunately her elderly parents had requisitioned Janet, the local builder's wife as her godmother. So for many years she joined their large family on cycling and camping holidays in Cornwall, Wales and Scotland. This was much more fun than home even thought it did not endear her to her status-conscious classmates holidaying in the Mediterranean.

Proximity

The principal reason Emma's parents selected Janet as godmother was her demonstrable skills at "stepping into the breach" whenever a crisis loomed. When Mrs Mills was rushed to hospital Janet effortlessly scooped up child and dog, squeezed them in somewhere, and didn't complain when they were forced to remain with her for two months. Emma's parents are of a gloomy disposition, convinced that fatal car accidents lurk round every corner, and although the long-term care of Emma would have been left in the hands of her capable but distant uncle, they wanted someone close to home who could pick up the pieces in the immediate aftermath.

With so many people moving for work reasons having a godparent living within striking distance can be a real benefit. Supporting the parents in the upbringing of the godchild can be quite practical for a godparent nearby. As the godchild grows up they can stay with the godparent / godparent's family so the parents can go away or just have a break. It's difficult for the godparent in another country to perform such a role.

Faith

The parents need to decide how important faith is and whether the parents want it to play a significant role in the godparent/godchild relationship. In some denominations, selecting at least one godparent of the same denomination will be mandatory. If this is the case, attempts should be made to find someone who is meaningful rather than having the obligatory Catholic, asked at the last minute, as godparent number five. This is a personal view, but to have least one godparent of reasonable religious or spiritual conviction, will add an important dimension to the child's development. Chapter 8 looks at this area in more detail.

Special needs

If a child has special needs, it would be consoling to think one may have met people in the same boat. It might be good idea to look among fellow-rowers for a godparent with direct experience of the child's condition or similar condition.

Single parents may want to beef up the complement of godparents of the sex of the absent parent.

Think twice

Asking two people who are married to each other to each to be godparents may be another case of short-changing a child and can be fraught with difficulty. Although it may solve the temporary problem of rivalry between the spouses, it is reasonable to assume that the spouse of a godparent will inevitably become involved anyway.

David and Victoria chose one single friend and both the members of two couples to be the godparents – effectively getting five godparents rather than three. This worked remarkably well as each member of the couple felt chosen and involved.

Nicky keeps a log of the birthdays of Connor's godchildren as well as her own, so that they are all looked after, whilst Connor mends the bicycles of all their combined godchildren.

Jake and Helen asked married friends to be godparents to Nora, but then they got divorced. Nora's birthdays, confirmation, and any other significant event are now a nightmare as Kathy and Peter refuse to be in the same room as each other. They both vie for Nora's attention in the same way as they do their own children, so if one godparent is invited to tea and the other not, the recriminations are endless.

Discussions with potential godparents

When inviting someone to become a godparent, it is important to do so in a way that does not require an immediate answer. Should one write, e-mail telephone or sms? There is no hard and fast rule: a letter allows the recipient to react privately, and take time to respond. It might be construed as a somewhat formal approach, and if the recipient takes a long time to respond, the parents are left wondering if the letter went astray, or whether the recipient is away or simply disinterested. A telephone call, on the other hand, conveys the immediate enthusiasm of the invitation but puts the prospective godparent on the spot. Ideally the telephone call or letter should be an initiation of discussions complete with permission to defer a definite response. Knee-jerk reactions to invitations may subsequently be regretted.

It is probably a good idea to have some discussion prior to firm "appointment" and "acceptance". The parents may think they have a reasonable idea on a prospective godparent's views on life, but an assumptions check may reveal otherwise. They may be pleasantly surprised to find how seriously the role is being taken or horrified to find that the prospective godparent has an allergy to children.

Topics covered will vary depending on the parents and prospective godparent, and it should be the godparent who is given the opportunity to outline their envisaged role. The godparent may be very clear in his own mind that whilst he is useless at remembering birthdays, he will be delighted to act as independent ombudsman in disputes between adolescent and parents. In the meantime he may also turn out to be a maestro at building airfix models of Hurricanes and Spitfires.

In reality, though, some godparents may not be good at birthdays, toddler entertainment or theme parks. It is useful to know this in advance and to ascertain whether the child's parents will mind, and whether the child will be affected if he does not always get a birthday present on time. If the godparent expects to encourage and stimulate the child in other ways - educationally, spiritually or morally - then he will be a good candidate and more likely to feel comfortable with his role having discussed it. He may also feel less embarrassed about giving the child "unbirthday" presents.

Daniel was discussing with his friend Alec why his godmother was better than Alec's. His final trump card was played when he pointed out that his godmother never remembered his birthday and that instead he received presents at the most unusual times of the year.

Issues of morality or faith, particularly if the parents have strong views, should be fully explored. If strongly held views are incompatible, and the potential godparent cannot in all conscience toe the parents' "party line", then it is probably unwise for the godparenthood to proceed. Better that than for confusion of the child and battles at a later date if his parents and godparent diametrically oppose each other. Diversity of views, however, should be welcomed - the child will be able to choose from a moral range but within a framework of individuals concerned for the godchild's well being.

Right to decline

Godparents should only accept if:

- they want to become godparent to the child;
- they feel they can satisfy the requirements of the role to their own standards;
- they feel they can meet the expectations of the parents.

Parents should respect a person's decision to decline the role, not take it personally and not automatically expect good reasons. A prospective godparent may decline because he or she has too many godchildren already. Regarding how many godchildren one can have, there is no rule on what the maximum number should be, it is entirely personal. However, not everyone has the capacity for 15 like Aunt Sybil.

On her 70th birthday Aunt Sybil invited all her 15 godchildren to join her with their partners on a boat down the Thames. They traveled from all over the world and 14 made it.

It is also possible, although harder to admit, that an invited prospective godparent may expect to be invited to fulfil that role in the future by other friends to whom he is more closely connected. It is important, whilst disappointed, not to feel put out when this occurs – it is unlikely to mean that he does not like or care for the person making the request, it may just be that his sense of obligation is stronger to the other parties.

Distance may also be a disincentive to godparenting. Some people feel that it is important to get to know their godchildren well and will therefore mind if they are not within easy access of them, even if the parents don't.

Some people are reluctant to become godparents because they are atheist or agnostic in matters of faith. We address this area in chapter 8. If this is not of concern it may be possible to allay their fears, but they may still be found squeamish about the vows they are expected to make at the christening in the traditional service. Adopting one of the alternative ceremonies in this book may solve this issue.

It is important that the prospective godparent is permitted to air their concerns and given time to make their decision.

One of their concerns might be that they will be expected to reciprocate the request when they have children, and whilst they are delighted to godparent your child, they have already mentally earmarked others to godparent their children. If this is an issue, discussion may result in an outcome satisfactory to all parties.

Never too late to ask

For a parent with godparentless children it is never too late to ask – assuming of course that the children aren't in their 20's. In some cases it might be wise to involve the children in the decision.

When Tim at the age of 10 won a chorister's scholarship his parents discovered to their horror that the boy needed to be baptized in order to take up the place. Consulting the son a shortlist of candidates for the position of godparent was drawn up and the son rang those identified if they would become his godparents. Ringing up the unsuspecting godfather Greg was asked, "Are you a Christian and will you be my godfather?" Greg, taken aback by so direct an approach answered in the affirmative and accepted.

Naomi aged 16 decided to get christened and wanted Constance as a godmother. Wishing to follow the proper etiquette she got her father to ask.

Chapter 5

MEETING THE CHALLENGE

The godparent's perspective

"It is better to give than to receive- but its quite tough being on the giving end for the best part of 15 years." said godmother Jane being able to look back and say it was worth the sacrifice now that she enjoys a close friendship with godchild Haley aged 23.

From our research, most people would like to be a godparent. Most people feel it is a great honour to be asked as it affirms the affection / respect in which one is held by the parents of the child. Assuming one regards children generally as a blessing, rather than a curse, then a godchild is a particular blessing and being a godparent confers considerable benefits onto the godparent as well as the godchild. It is no surprise that those who are active godparents feel grateful for the privilege, and speak of their godchildren with delight.

In welcoming the godparent onto private territory, the godparenting framework affords the godparent the pleasure of giving (emotionally, temporally or spiritually) to a child without the worry that such affection may be intrusive. Most of us live in a society where we tread carefully with respect to each other's privacy, and because everyone perceives everyone else to be busy and preoccupied, involvement with others can be sub-consciously rationed. Yet there are parts of us which long to feel more deeply engaged with others in our social networks, and each of us may hold hidden unutilized capacity for greater human participation/involvement. The channels for such engagement are not always obvious, and involve elaborate social minuets around who invites who to what and how often. The invitation to godparent an offspring cuts through such social niceties, sets them aside and is a declaration of permission to become engaged in the family's affairs on a much deeper level. Other than the invitation between two adults to a committed partnership, there is probably no greater permission to involvement in an intimate area of people's lives than the invitation to godparent an offspring. Godparents are chosen – family are not.

In addition to this fundamental affirmation of a friendship between parents and the godparent, it introduces a potential new friendship between godparent and godchild. For the childfree - and there are increasing numbers of adults who find themselves intentionally or unintentionally in this category - it provides an important and valuable link to the next generation. For those with children, it expands family connections which may benefit their own children.

There are also "costs" to becoming a godparent, although these costs (in business speak) should represent "investments" in the relationship rather than costs to be written off:

- Financial – presents, lots of them, although we strongly advocate that financial value is unimportant if the giver's resources are limited.
- Time – often under-estimated, but the fuller the time investment, the greater the rewards.
- Emotional – it will not always be sunny teas and easy playtimes, there may be some heart ache too.

Accepting the role

Accepting such a role is a commitment, albeit pleasurable, and the process of acceptance is a mirror image of the process of selection discussed in the previous chapter. Potential godparents should ask themselves:

- What do they believe godparenthood entails?
- Do they want to be a godparent at all? Not everyone wants to be a godparent. It is perfectly acceptable not

to want it.

- Do they believe they can satisfy the requirements of the role to somewhere near their own standards? No-one is expected to be perfect – there is no point turning down the role just because the potential godparent's diary system for birthdays is unreliable.
- What are the expectations of the parents? They may differ significantly from the godparent's expectations, in which case it is best that these are aired up front.
- How do they feel about their relationship with the parents of the child, and therefore their potential relationship with the child? Is it close enough? Do they want to be friends with the parents for the rest of their lives?
- Are there other practical considerations e.g. geography, other commitments, which might mitigate against acceptance of the role, even if they wanted it?
- Are there spiritual convictions that prevent the godparent from being able to accept? (Although spiritual convictions need not be a barrier to accepting godchildren of a different faith, not everyone might be comfortable with this in which case if there is any doubt, it may be better for all parties if the role is declined.)

Requirements of godparenting

(i) Contact

The biggest requirement is an interest in the child. If the potential godparent is not, deep down, really interested, it is probably best to pass on the invitation. Not everyone is interested in other people's children or a particular child – it is better to be honest about this than take on a chore. Godparenting does not need to be a chore – if it feels like a chore, the potential godparent should leave it to someone else.

Time is important, but if the potential godparent is short of time in the normal course of events, he may be able to compensate for this in some other way – e.g. spending occasional quality time with the child when the child is older. Ideally godparents should see their godchildren regularly, but in reality this may not be feasible. Once or twice a year with a child who lives at the other end of the country, (together with other communication by card, letter, phone or email), may be what is realistic. If the child lives in a different country, a visit once every few years may be all that is possible – finance permitting. The key is that having seen his godparent once in a while, the child can hope to expect to see his godparent again at some future date. If a potential godparent is uncomfortable about how much time they can commit, it is a good idea to discuss this with the child's parents who may be relaxed about this. It is also important to remember that life goes in phases and if the problem is the godparent's own struggles with parenting toddlers, this may ease as time goes by allowing more time for godchildren later.

Jerry's parents lived in Peru. Anna was invited to be Jerry's godmother whilst on a posting there, but as she already had six godchildren in the UK and was shortly due to move back there, after much heart-searching she declined. By her calculations she would realistically only see Jerry once every three years – the parents didn't mind, but she did. Also she was worried about how her commitment to Jerry would encroach upon her already stretched commitments to the other six godchildren. Fortunately she knew that a mutual friend was unexpectedly keen to become a godparent, and so it seemed a much better solution that he godparent Jerry instead of Anna. Anna has in any case remained in close touch and sees Jerry once every few years, enjoying a special friendship but without failing her commitments.

Nancy on the other hand declined to be Laura's godmother because at the time she had couple of toddlers of her own who were driving her demented. When her own children had calmed down a few years later, and Laura's mother was diagnosed with cancer, Nancy bitterly regretted her earlier decision. She now had the time, and wished that she had taken on the responsibility to look out for Laura's well-being. In reality, she contributes anyway, but it doesn't feel the same.

Godparents can themselves set a minimum target of contacts per year – visit, phone call, e-mail, sms or post-card / letter. Ultimately though the godparent has to be able to meet the bare minimum of his own standards – or the old demon of godparenting, "guilt", will reappear.

(ii) Birthdays and what interests the child

If the potential godparent is worried about remembering birthdays et al there are a number of ways to overcome this which we explore in Chapter 6. In any case, birthday presents are not the be-all and end-all in the relationship. Discuss upfront with the parents, so that expectations are managed and there is no fall-out if birthdays are forgotten. Whilst the godchild will love to receive birthday presents, if expectations are managed carefully it will not be the end of the world if this does not occur, and the godchild should anyway reap non-material rewards from the relationship instead.

In Chapter 6 we also discuss a range of ideas for presents and activities to do with any godchild. It is always satisfying when the godchild shares an interest with the godparent. However, particularly in the years up to 16 the godparent is likely to end up going to things or giving presents revolving around the child's interests. Some godparents when arranging to see the godchild will ask the child what they would like to do. If their passion is train spotting a visit to a train station maybe the most life-giving thing to do. If playing gameboy or watching a sport is currently important to the godchild then godparents showing an interest are more likely to build rapport and a relationship.

(iii) Expectations

A potential godparent may find it helpful to discuss with the parents why they have been selected, and through the process identify the particular attributes the parents appreciate about the godparent which they feel may be beneficial to the child's development in due course.

(iv) Relationship with the parents

It is very helpful if the potential godparent really likes the parents of the godchild. This may sound obvious, but it is surprising how some godparents admit that they were never really sure why they were asked to be a godparent, particularly as they felt they had little in common or did not particularly get on with the child's parents. However, it is not an absolute prerequisite to really like the child's parents, if the potential godparent feels able and willing to care about the child notwithstanding.

Melissa always felt ambivalent about the Shillings. He was a ne'er-do-well and she was nice but unexciting. Her heart sank when they asked her to be Keith's godmother. But she accepted - she reasoned that although she was not wealthy herself, by comparison to the Shillings she was as rich as Croesus and unless she accepted Keith was never going to have a bicycle. Keith's father, as expected, deserted the marital home, and it seemed unlikely that the boy would ever do well. But Melissa conferred praise whenever she could, had him to tea, kept in touch, sent encouraging notes, and against the expectations of many Keith ended up with decent qualifications and a respectable job. Melissa also ended up being really rather fond of Keith: him + wife + sprogs beam down at her from a photo on the mantelpiece and they all pop in on the old dear on the way to his mum's.

It is important that any potentially contentious issues (religion, envisaged role) are discussed with the parents prior to acceptance. It may be straightforward however. Accept as quickly as possible so that the parents can plan christenings etc – sitting on the invitation for protracted periods is not helpful.

Bringing up children for most parents is a kaleidoscope of emotions - tough, challenging, exhilarating, exhausting, magical and frustrating. Godparents who are able to offer support and encouragement to the parents for the duration will be playing an invaluable function. Feeling that someone else is sharing the load and interested in them and the child can be of real benefit. This is particularly the case when the godchild concerned turns out to be a hyper-active, attention seeking creature that no one is quite sure where he came from unless it was Zorg.

Declining the role

The previous chapter explored the godparent's right to decline the role, but still parents may be very hurt if a invited godparent declines. This is no reason not to decline if the godparent is convinced he does not want the job. Where possible it may be helpful to explain why whilst reassuring the parents of their continued esteem. Continuing to take an interest in the child and even giving presents from time to time may serve to mollify parties.

It is important that the declining party uses language that stresses their conviction that acceptance is inappropriate: "I don't have enough time" might lead to protracted negotiations about how much time is required, whereas "I really feel I'll give insufficient time and end up neglecting my duties" is harder to argue with.

It's never too late to improve - the reformed godparent

For the majority of godparents who feel they don't perform the role very well the only way to rectify the situation is to act. Prevarication doesn't work. A few steps that could be considered include:

(i) Resolve – remembering the child's birthday is a good start, if necessary double check with the parents that the date you think it is (wild guesses permitted) is correct and record it somewhere.

Having forgotten Luca's birthday for the second year running, godmother Meg sent a gift with a card saying that Luca was fully entitled to sack her as an inadequate godmother. More grateful to hear that his mother's former nursing colleague hadn't completely fallen off the face of the earth the 8 year old godchild magnanimously decided to retain her services.

(ii) Speak – with the parents and godchild if old enough and find out how the whole family is. The godparent can admit that they feel they have not been doing a very good job of godparenting. The godparent can ask the parents and ask them to provide updates.

Once the ice has been broken, the godparent can now discuss with the parents what they would like him to do now that he has recovered his resolve.

(iii) Arrange visits either to the child, or for the child and/or family to come and stay.

(iv) Start to record presents and contacts. If presents are too difficult maybe set up a bank standing order.

(v) Celebrate the renewed contact and resumed journey with a glass of something – water, champagne or whatever - ideally with the godchild's family.

Chapter 6

THE PRACTICAL ASPECTS OF GODPARENTING

Tips to make the logistics of godparenting easier

Anybody with godchildren knows that one of the hardest aspects can be simply staying in touch and remembering special occasions.

The harsh reality is that the godchild/godparent relationship is like all relationships - it needs investing in if it is to grow. The additional challenge for this relationship is that typically the godparent is making the running for a significant period of time (possibly up to 16 years) before there is much appreciation/response from the godchild.

Given that this is a test of character and discipline most effective godparents have no choice but to adapt a "willful" approach and plan to do certain things at certain times to ensure they do make the regular investment required. This selfless giving is not always easy, but is the essence of the godparent demonstrating and communicating unconditional support and acceptance.

Keeping in touch is vital to validate such unconditional support. This is a two-way process and needs parents to play their part in keeping the godparent up to date with the child's progress. "Have you written to say thank you?" reminders from the parents to the child are also helpful.

If appropriate, and maybe where the godparents are in another country, parents can also help by sending copies of school reports. This won't be to everybody's taste but some godparents will appreciate the gesture and it does have the benefit of involving the godparent in the child's development and hearing what the school has to say. Knowing how the child is doing at school can only increase the godparents understanding of the child and how they are getting on. It may also serve a purpose in inspiring ideas on how they can be involved in encouraging the child's interests.

Yvonne's school report said "Yvonne displays a growing appreciation of colour and light and shows promise in her painting. It is unfortunate that she has decided to take up science A levels instead of arts." Alice,Yvonne's godmother also had an artistic bent and on reading the above rang Yvonne to invite her to come with her to one day art course near her home.

Diarise

The advent of the electronic diary has been extremely helpful to godparents who have decided that remembering Christmas and birthdays is important. Reminders a few weeks in advance (most electronic diaries can have a recurring annual entry) can allow the godparent time to get organized. For those without electronic gizmos, use a diary or calendar with birthdays to remember recorded. It may be possible to diaries the godchild's birthday a few weeks in advance and then communicate with the parents or godchild to find out what the child might like. Alternatively all godchildren can get a present on a particular date e.g. Easter.

Jonny who has ten (godchildren) couldn't cope with remembering all his ten godchildrens' birthdays so decided to send all of them a card / presents on his own birthday.

Some godparents don't remember the child's birthday but remember the child's christening date. This can be particularly useful for godchildren born near Christmas/new year. The christening date becomes a type of official birthday. The advantage of this is that it does reinforce the "special" relationship of godparent/godchild. Even so godparents adopting this approach should deploy an early warning system.

Willie always received a card from his godfather Arthur on 16 June and not in April when his birthday occurred. When Willie later studied in South Africa and supported the struggle against Apartheid the fact that his christening day was also Soweto day had particular significance.

Making regular dates for making telephone calls or sending e-mails to a godchild is greatly helped if put in the diary.

Contact levels

Ideally godparents might see their godchild at least once or twice a year, where this is practical. Again, ideally godparents would communicate with their godchild on their birthday, Christmas and for some, christening day. In addition to the above we would encourage godparent to communicate with their godchildren at other times and not restrict contact to these events.

Postcards sent from holiday, places of interest or even business travel is a very useful and convenient way to maintain such contact and for the child is very exciting. Although becoming a lost art, letter writing can still be a wonderful form of communication and always a delight to receive particularly if an aerogramme.

Jean would periodically send a postcard of a painting or sculpture to her goddaughter Clair when she visited a gallery in nearby Edinburgh – particularly when she thought Clair would appreciate the piece of work concerned.

The electronic age has reduced excuses for godparents not staying in touch: email and digital photography are excellent tools for the purpose, and as increasingly children have their own mobile phones SMS or texting is also a fun way of communicating.

Dictation into a cassette or CD (not everyone's cup of tea) is an effective alternative, particularly when distances are an issue.

Awareness of important events – exams, new schools, achievements – all help to cement the relationship through good luck messages or rewards for effort.

Jason, Andy's godfather, remembered that his godson was taking an exam and sent a good luck card. When Andy passed, he informed Jason that miracles still happened and Jason sent a congratulatory cheque.

Remember your will

If one wants to include godchildren in the will and allocate chattels to them it will be necessary to draft an intent of this and communicate this to the lawyer and the executors. A letter of wishes may be used for this, although as we saw with the Princess of Wales's letter of wishes, unless all executors know about it and have bought into its contents, its true intentions may not be fulfilled in full. A codicil is legally binding, and if the godparent is leaving cash to the child much easier for the executors to follow through. (Unless in the will or codicil proper, the beneficiaries would have to pass cash to the godchildren as a gift, which may, depending on size of gift, have tax implications).

Freddy's godmother Joy left him some money in her will. As a single woman having prayed and shown concern for him throughout his life Freddy was extremely grateful for the love he had received. Now that he going to be ordained he decided to use the money to buy a desk at which he could write his sermons and pray. He thought this appropriate as he didn't think he would be following this career path had it not been for his godmother.

Foolproof fallbacks

Time, distance and the pace of life mitigate against godparents finding time to invest in their godchildren. A standing order to a dedicated savings accounts is a safe fallback position, particularly if the godparent remembers a timely card or email. (The co-operation of the child's parents to open an appropriate account will probably be necessary as opening accounts in the names of third parties is increasingly complex given current anti-money-laundering legislation). Although somewhat impersonal, children often enjoy the accumulation of wealth that can then be spent on a large item of their choice when older. For child-free godparents the challenge of what an eleven-year-old might crave is avoided.

Present giving and activities

HEALTH WARNING

BEFORE SUGGESTING PRESENT AND GIFT IDEAS THERE IS A GENERAL CAVEAT THAT PRESENT GIVING IS NOT A REQUIRED ASPECT OF GODPARENTING. THE ROLE OF THE GODPARENT IS FAR MORE SIGNIFICANT THAN BEING A BENEVOLENT GIFT DISPENSER. PRESENT GIVING IS NOT ESSENTIAL.

Far more important is being concerned for them, interested in their growth and development and making periodic contact. Moreover, the tenet that it's the thought that counts holds true in an ever increasing materialistic global village. If you thought that your godchild would appreciate something that cost very little that is of equal value to something that may have cost a bodily appendage.

Godparenting does not and should not require a minimum disposable godspend income. The only requirement is love, interest and concern for the godchild however shown and communicated.

Having said that, however, most godparents, like most parents, do give presents from time to time. We have made some practical suggestions as to what to give and what to do with godchildren at various ages. The ideas are by no means exhaustive, but is based on suggestions by a gratitude of godparents. They will hopefully provide a pool of ideas to draw upon and stimulate godparents wanting to send gifts or arrange events over the course of the relationship.

Godmother Beryl gave Christmas presents if she found something she liked. Sometimes she would give a tip if she had the cash but seldom regularly.

If possible we would also recommend that godparents of a particular child are in touch with each other and liaise on presents. A godmother with a fertile imagination for her goddaughter can feed a godfather who is stuck with ideas, and vice versa. It also provides an opportunity for godparents to discuss the child's progress and any issues of concern.

If godchildren are of similar ages it is nice to introduce them to each other from an early age. As godchildren get older, they can be introduced regardless of age. An annual godchildren's lunch or dinner could be a delightful social event, whilst broadening the godchildren's own social networks. It may even be possible at some point to get all the godchildren together for a longer period.

Once a year David gets all his godchildren (six) together and takes them off on a walk or a picnic. This has become an annual event all the godchildren look forward to.

Whatever you do, try and discuss present ideas with the parents ahead of time and keep a record of presents given. Keeping a record of what is given, and reaction if any, will enable godparents to avoid giving the same present twice. If an earlier present to an older godchild was a success, it may suit another one later.

Presents and activities

What not to do

It is probably better not to send fad gifts, which are out of date.

Despite the temptation it is probably better to get a mix between the totally frivolous and the very worthy type of presents. A child receiving only worthy presents could be forgiven for seeing the godparent on a mission of godchild improvement.

Godmother Angela was known for her outlandish presents including a lice comb and prints of her own works of art.

What to definitely do

If one records the date of birth of the godchild it should be possible to avoid sending gifts for a younger age than the godchild actually is. Make sure, however that the date is recorded somewhere sensible such as an address book.

Mary, the godchild, always received a card one year younger than she was – throughout her life.

Rachel received dolls house items from her godmother even when she was in her teens!

Baby 0-4 and christening

Traditional christening presents:
Silver napkin ring - engraved
Silver christening quaiche – engraved (ie small bowl)
Wine or port to "lay down" particularly if the year of the child's birth is a good vintage
Jewellery (antique or modern) for girls, some may favour crosses or St Christopher's – something involving the girl's birthstone?
Cuff links for boys
Cotton handkerchiefs with embroidered initials
Children's bible
Adult bible
Book of prayers
Waiting list (if you can get on it) for MCC, Glyndebourne, anything else that interests you
Life memberships such as National Trust are a nice idea

Less traditional christening presents:
Art, sculpture or photography

Patricia scored such a hit with a bronze for her goddaughter which quintupled in value in as many years that the mother offered to return it.

Poetry anthology – such as Wavell's "Other Men's Flowers", (only available second hand in hard back)
Rare books
Art /antiques/rugs
Foreign bibelots

Many bookshops stocking children's books now categorise the books into different age groups. Shop assistants are usually knowledgeable about what is popular and can be of great help when selecting. Also check booklists such as Penguin, Waterstones, Walker Books etc.

General presents:
Mobile
Soft toys
Cloth or board books
Wooden toys/building bricks/Duplo
Nativity set for Christmas, gradually building up the set (some godparents find nativity figures from around the world)
National Savings Certificates or equivalent
Bank account with cash to go with
Clothes (although remember a babygro will only last a few weeks and anything else a few months)

Childhood 5-11

Games associated with play / exploration:
Board games (Monopoly, chess, draughts, Risk)
Lego
Train set
Doll's House
Airfix model
Scrap books and albums (even stamps)
Art paper, paints, pencils, crayons particularly if the godchild is artistic
Dressing up costumes
Christmas decorations, especially from abroad
Football team, rugby team shirts

Godfather Bryan gives his godson a pair of goalkeeping gloves every year – each year the next size up.

Sports equipment, cricket bats, cricket stumps, football boots, balls, tennis rackets, badminton, squash, basketball, etc
Kite
Camera (shoot and click) / disposable black and white
For school:
Smart pencil case, school bag, pens/pencils (fancy ones)
Your old satchel (if appropriate)
Diaries, notebooks etc for girls

Music: lessons, or if you are able lend or help acquire instruments, instrument accessories (e.g. cases) and music books

Books:
Books with tapes
Books: Classics such as Hobbit, Green Knowe series, R Dahl, Swallows and Amazons, Stig of the Dump, Treasure Island, Robinson Crusoe, My Life and other animals, Emile and the Detectives, Moomintroll books
Books by more recent authors such as J K Rowling, Anthony Horrowitz, Jacqueline Wilson, Malary Blackman, Ann Fine, Philip Pullman, Roald Dahl etc.
Relevant books on faith
Children's poetry anthologies
Children's Treasury of literature
Flower Fairy Books – as there are several in the series can cover couple of years' presents
Reference books or CD roms: e.g. Atlas

General presents:
Bicycle/bicycle accessories – speedometer, bag, repair kits
Compass
Watch
Subscriptions for comics, specialist magazines,
Computer games

Generic:
Tokens – book, film, CD, theater

Activities:
Bake cakes together
Colour books together
Museum visits
National Trust, English Heritage and private stately homes (many have child-friendly events days)
Art gallery visits
Wintershall – nativity play at Christmas or Life of Christ in summer, whole day, bring picnic
York Mystery Plays

Legoland, Alton Towers, Bradford National Photography Museum, steam rallies
Theatre/shows e.g. Lion King, Chitty Chitty Bang Bang
Visit to local toy or bookshop (e.g. Hamleys) and godchild chooses something
Children's Proms
Ballet –Nutcracker Suite, Swan Lake
Cinema
Riding lessons
Skating
Pottery
Walking
Camping
Youth hostelling
Vintage Silverstone
Sports fixtures - football, rugby, cricket

Unusual:
Pets (unless you want to become a dogparent or end up in the dogbox suggest you check with the parents first)
Invite them to join you on holiday
Invite them for a weekend or week at your home
Give holiday money - some people find out what the normal pocket money is and multiply that by the number of days the godchild will be away on holiday to work out what to give.

Charities:
Sponsorship of a child in a developing country (child becomes pen-pal)
Godparent will give x to a charity for the next 5 years - godchild chooses
Adopting an animal in a wildlife sanctuary
Send a Cow or equivalent

Confirmation/First Communion

Crucifix
Up to date Bible e.g The Message
Prayer book and other book relating to faith
Selection of prayers

Spiritual classics – Brother Lawrence, Thomas a Kempis, Pascal's "Penses",
Boenhoeffer - Letters from Prison, Cost of Discipleship
C S Lewis – Four Loves, Mere Christianity, Screwtape Letters
R Forster – Celebration of Discipline
(Some of these books may be for future appreciation)

Teenage 12-18
General:
If in doubt send a cheque / postal order /transfer money to an account in their or the parents' name
Rucksack
Swiss Army Knife
Leatherman
Shaving kit
Sleeping bag (down)
Walking boots
Climbing wall sessions (particularly if you do it together but see section on making a will first!)
Tent
Wallet
Travel alarm clocks
Sewing box
Jewellery box
Clothes – bought with the godchild!
Computer games
Games e.g. bridge, cribbage, twister, etc
Bicycle/bicycle accessories - lights and reflectors, helmet
Nicely bound note-books e.g. Moleskin
Ipods
Mobile phones
Gadgets

Books:
Books about their special interests
Classics e.g. Long walk to Freedom (Mandela)
Reference books
Dictionary of quotations, literature

School / educational:
Subsidising educational activities, e.g. travel to French exchange, school activities
Theatre – Shakespeare
Concerts, films
Art materials – easel, papers, brushes etc
Music lessons
Riding lessons
Lessons about anything they enjoy (martial arts, pottery, rock climbing)

Activities:
Music – Dartington (participatory music festival)
Visit local museums e.g. York Railway museum
Visit local National Trust / English Heritage stately homes
Attending summer camps – outdoor activities, Christian (e.g. CYFA, Scripture Union)
Major sporting events (if you can get tickets)
Walking holiday/camping
W/e to European city
Visit other place of worship.
Camping with godchild / all godchildren
Invite godchild for a weekend of doing nothing in particular – mooching, shopping
Ten pin bowling
Quad biking
Go karting
Jet skiing
Para gliding
Fly-fishing
Diving
Snooker / pool

Unusual:
Commission godchild to design / make Christmas cards for you one year
Pets

Generic:
Subscriptions e.g. National Geographic, specialist magazines

Tokens – book, film, CD, theater

Late teens early 20's

A godparent may want to ensure that a lump sum goes to a godchild on their eighteenth or twenty-first birthday. Even if the child is still young, you may want to set aside the cash now in a separate account and inform the parents of its existence. It is then ready for transfer on the godchild's birthday. With luck the godchild will already have a bank account – setting up bank accounts on anothers' behalf can be a cumbersome and difficult process.

General:
Cufflinks (if they are likely to wear double cuff shirts one day)
Anything to do with a Gap Year if appropriate– cash, flight tickets, kit not previously given
Courses – music, art, wine tasting, bridge
Subscriptions – National Geographic, Economist, The Week
Useful kit for university/first home – tools, bedding, kitchen utensils, Anglepoise lamp
computer software, computer, mobile phone, organiser
Drinking kit
Driving lessons
Gliding lessons
Dinner jacket
Smart frock / clothes / coat
Hat
Tokens and cash

Books:
Second hand books, poetry anthologies,

Activities:
Glynebourne, Covent Garden, Proms, Jazz Cultural festivals
Festivals – Glastonbury, Greenbelt, Womad,
Book Festivals - Edinburgh, Cheltenham, Hay-on-Wye
Sports camps
Sports lessons e.g. Tennis

Travel:
Sponsor or go together to monastic retreats, Mt Athos (godfathers and godsons only)
Walking holidays
Trip to the Antarctic
Retreat

Beyond 21

Household items
Evening classes (preferably fun)
Visits to health spa
Sporting equipment e.g. golf clubs

Chapter 7

RELATIONSHIP WITH THE PARENTS AND OTHER GODPARENTS

Godparents and parents

Choosing godparents for a child implicitly tells all concerned that the parents would hope to maintain the relationship between themselves and the godparents. Other than marriage when best men and bridesmaids / ushers are chosen this is one of the few formal opportunities in life to recognize the significance of a particular friendship. This vote of appreciation carries with it the anticipation of maintaining the parent - godparent relationship.

Unsurprisingly, the research performed for this book confirms that an important element in the process of godparents feeling that they were making progress was maintaining the relationship with the parents. Where the original friendship continues the godparenting relationship with the child also tends to grow and be reinforced.

Support

The godparent can play an important role of supporting the parents in the difficult task of bringing up the godchild. Where logistics permit such support may be hands-on. Where distance is an issue the support is more likely to be emotional and through calls, writing and emails.

When visits can be arranged (in either direction) they feed the relationship and help everyone involved to be aware how the others are getting on.

Bringing up children is not easy and any part godparents can play in sharing the load or showing solidarity with the parents should be encouraged. Inviting the godchild for weekends or school holidays may give the parents a break as well as provide the chance for godparent and godchild to get to know each other better.

Unfortunately, however, there are three areas of relationship where disintigration can occur due to:

Distance

In our mobile age very often godparents or parents move around the country or the globe making it that much harder to stay in contact.

Jo and Mark have lived in Hong Kong for 7 years so haven't seen much of the boys' godparents. Being out of sight appears to have resulted in some of the godparents falling off the face of the earth.

When the parents no longer have the address of a godparent and the relationship has evaporated, unless someone resurrects the contact the godparent / godchild relationship is also likely to vanish.

Godfather Eric had lost contact with godson James until one day he noticed a photo on someone's fridge. Pointing out that this was his godson and expressing interest in what he was doing resulted in contact being re-established between godfather and godson.

Sometimes the godparents chosen may have been good friends when the child was born but over time both parties realize they have drifted apart and have less in common. Circumstance may bring people together but is may not necessarily be the basis for a long lasting friendship. In such situations parents may want to think about replacing the invisible godparent with another.

Falling out

Similar to drifting apart can be the situation where the godparent falls out with the parents or parent. In such a situation it might prove difficult for the godparent to continue contacting the godchild, particularly where any visits to the home could be awkward. However, in the same way divorced parents normally have access to the child it is still possible for the godparents to continue to see the child and build the relationship. A non- functioning relationship with the parents doesn't automatically mean the end of the godchild/ godparent relationship so long as the parents consent and can see the value of it. This can be even more important if a divorce is involved and the child needs even more affirmation and unconditional acceptance than ever.

Upbringing disputes

In some relationships surveyed, disputes have arisen between godparent and parents regarding the upbringing of the child. If the godparent fundamentally disagrees with the parents' approach on discipline or spoiling the child out of guilt for not spending sufficient time with the child, for example, the godparent may very well mention their concern and observations. If the parents can discuss the matter openly and together work out an approach all are happy with, or reconciled to, life should continue. Where however, defensiveness and anger are the outcome serious damage could be done. Given the godparents' commitment to the child's growth and development it is consistent with that concern to speak out rather than say nothing.

When Bill was thinking of leaving Karen for another woman the godmother Tess was devastated. In particular she was concerned about the impact it would have on her godson George, aged 6. Taking her courage in both hands she decided she had to confront Bill and talk it through. Three hours later after a difficult and emotional conversation the two emerged with their friendship intact and Bill resolved to stick with his marriage.

If the godparent feels he can't intervene, then he shouldn't flagellate himself. An alternative may be to canvass the opinions of co-godparents, and investigate whether there is another godparent who is better positioned to say something.

Godparents and other godparents

Often the godparents are chosen from various episodes in the parents' lives. Consequently the godparents, although having the parents and now the godchild in common, do not necessarily know each other.

Depending on chemistry it may be possible to exchange contact details with the other godparents with a view to getting in touch at some point. This could be useful when buying presents and the godparents join forces. It could also help if a crisis arises where two or three heads are better than one.

Chapter 8

GODPARENTING FOR CHRISTIANS, ATHEISTS & THOSE IN BETWEEN

Spiritual development

This book encourages all godparents regardless of their own religious persuasion to encourage the godchild to appreciate the place of faith in the world. Helping them see how faith has influenced ideas, history, great writing, architecture, music and art is an important element in the godchild's understanding of the world in which they live. All this is part of helping initiate the godchild and guiding them into fulfilling lives. This approach underlies what follows where we look at how godparents of different ideologies can apply the role.

When Patrick was feeling less than inspired with church his godfather Eric encouraged him to persevere and pray- or find a new faith community. His constant warning was not to become a spiritual island.

(i) The Christian godparent

For the Christian godparent the role as it relates to spiritual development will involve a desire to see the godchild come to believe in Christ themselves and find a faith of their own. Such an aspiration will be part and parcel of the concern for the child's growth and maturity. Through building up a relationship with the child and becoming a sympathetic adult and trusted mentor the influence of the godparent in matters temporal and spiritual should be established.

The promises made during the traditional baptism service serve as a guide in terms of this aspect of godparenting. In particular responding in the affirmative to the question posed by the priest of, "*Will you draw them by your example into the community of faith and walk with them in the way of Christ*?", will challenge the Christian godparent in their conduct and encourage them to walk with the godchild in the way of Christ.

When Kevin was baptized his godmother gave the parents a sealed envelope for Kevin to be opened when he was an adult. This letter was opened 15 years later and set out the hopes the godmother had for him ultimately finding a faith of his own. Over the years the prayers, interest and generosity shown to Kevin by his godmother went hand in hand with her desire to see him experience God for himself. Had she died in the meantime her hopes at the time of baptism would still have been communicated at a later date in Kevin's life and would have left a type of spiritual legacy.

Behind the scenes the challenge for the godparent is to regularly pray for the growth and development of the child – that he or she would mature emotionally and reach their God-given potential. For centuries praying for others has been seen as a constructive activity and of direct benefit to the person being prayed for. If the godparent can find out what specific things need praying for that will be better than the general type of praying.

Practically, trying to remember to pray for the godchild will be an important part of performing the role. In the same way that natural parents often say that not a day goes by without them thinking about their children and wondering how they are if godparents can cultivate a similar approach and bring the child to God's attention such daily activity will reap its rewards.

The fact that Ben's godmother had prayed for him every day since he was born was of immense importance to Ben. Not only did it demonstrate his godmother's concern and commitment to him but provided great support through the ups and downs of life. It also created a sense of godmother and godson looking to God for strength and guidance as Ben came to major crossroads and decision times.

Godmother Connie tries to remember to pray for her godchildren – give them Grace, oh God, or sometimes more specific.

A key element in helping the godchild discover their own faith and growing up spiritually will be through the godparent sharing their own journey of faith and life with the godchild. The godparent will look to encourage the child to discover the relevance of the Christian faith for themselves. Through being honest and open the godparent can discuss with the godchild the ups and downs of following Christ, the challenges and difficulties, the joys and sorrows, the sense of purpose and desolation: in sum the whole spectrum of the life of faith as clearly represented in the Psalms. If the godparent can show that to follow Christ is the way to know God and find fulfillment in life, this will speak volumes to the godchild.

As Sarah grew up her friendship with her godmother developed. They would explore hedgerows and forests together and go on outings to the countryside. The godmother would explain on occasion how God had played an important part in her own life and how she had made decisions at the crossroads in her life with prayer and trust. When Sarah was struggling with the concept of confirmation, which the school chaplain was encouraging, the godmother discussed the matter, agreeing with the significance of the ceremony but supporting her only to go ahead if she really did want to confirm her loyalty to Christ and desire to follow him. Two years later Sarah did get confirmed out of a personal conviction that this was what she wanted.

Over time and particularly when the godchild is making important decisions it may be of great value if the godparent initiates praying for the situation together. This not only brings God directly into the equation but also can serve to deepen the relationship between godparent and godchild.

As Tony grew up he and his godmother would talk about the different challenges they were both facing and would pray for each other. Not so much a case of role reversal but the developing of a mutually supportive friendship with God at the heart.

(ii) The agnostic godparent

For the agnostic, participating in the ceremonies in the Appendix 1 and 2 should not be problematic. Agreeing to help the godchild develop spiritually will be something they can relate to and hope for. Providing exposure to different faiths and worldviews should not cause an agnostic any difficulties. As to what to reply when asked by the godchild what he or she actually believes, as with the ceremony that the godparent may have participated in, an honest response is best. The godparent can participate in the child's discovery of faith and discuss experiences and books read together. This also demonstrates that the godparent is on a spiritual journey and is still discovering / learning etc.

(iii) The atheistic godparent

The atheist, similar to the agnostic should be able to make the promises present in both ceremonies proposed in Appendix 1 and 2. The fact that faith has played an historic role in society may for the atheist demonstrate man's superstition and need to have a god of the gaps but should not prevent him or her assisting the godchild in understanding these matters. While he or she may profoundly disagree with Christian tenets, the likes of JS Bach attributed their motivation and gifts to God and devoted their output to him. Appreciation of such is not asking anyone to commit intellectual suicide. Encouraging the godchild to form their own views on life and faith should involve the atheist godparent in sharing their own perspective and challenging and respecting the godchild if he or she does develop a faith of their own.

If the child is to be baptized in a traditional ceremony the atheist godparent to be should discuss the matter with the parents and work out a common understanding. Parents and godparents may decide, as many do, to live with the contradiction of promising certain things but not believing in the God concerned. Alternatively the godparent to be may not attend the service or not reply to the questions posed. However, adopting an alternative ceremony, as suggested, rather than going along with the traditional ceremony should be considered if this is the case.

iv) Other faiths

Lastly, asking godparents of another faith will certainly broaden the godchild's godparenting in the spiritual sphere. The approach of such godparents should not be dissimilar to the above - encouragement of the child in his or her spiritual journey and sharing of one's own faith in the process. If the parents wish their child to be brought up in a particular faith this should be discussed and agreed with the invited godparent.

Parents coming from a faith with no tradition of godparenting will hopefully see the value of godparents and may be encouraged to initiate godparenting for their children.

Godmother Coleen had a Jewish godson and supposed that they worshiped the same God. Concerned that if she wasn't to be redundant as a godmother she challenging the godson for the lack of religious education when Samuel was 8 years old. Action was taken and she later attended Samuel's Bar Mitzvah in a ferocious feather bonnet - not wishing to be outdone by the Hassidic hats.

Chapter 9

GODCHILD IN CRISIS OR IN TROUBLE

Crises

It is sometimes the case that a godparent comes into his or her own during a crisis involving the godchild.

Heather's mother died after the war and shortly before Heather was due to get married. Godmother Eilleen stepped into the breach providing a family wedding dress and hosting the reception. As Heather's children grew up Eilleen continued to play an important role with the family regularly staying with her in the Lakes for holidays. The wedding dress now hangs in a local museum.

The statistics on prevalence of marital unhappiness, divorce, alcoholism, mental illness, other health problems, bereavement, or financial problems in the 21st century are depressing. Problems may be encountered within ones own household, and certainly within ones acquaintanceship. Any of these problems may well strike the family of a godchild.

If it is believed that there is a problem unfolding in the godchild's family as a friend of the family and godparent, the godparent will naturally be concerned. It is impossible to say what should be done in each situation. Nor will one response with one set of parents be appropriate to another. It maybe that having offered support the godparent has to sit back and wait to be asked to get involved. Being there and at the end of the phone may be all there is to do.

In other situations the godparent may be asked to get involved directly - possibly to speak with the godchild or may be to dig out what experts say on the issue at hand such as an unusual medical condition. Armed with information as to how a particular problem may manifest itself, how a child may react, and what types of behaviour indicate particular distress, one will be better prepared and better able to assist the parents in dealing with the situation as constructively and helpfully as possible.

When godchild Alan developed a rare failure to thrive illness strange marks appeared on his arms and legs. Inspired godmother Claire called them angel's kisses which transformed them from being worrisome to being treasured by Alan.

It is seldom appropriate, however, to confront a confused child with a direct "tell me your feelings" when you see them. Instead, children often want to know that if they need to talk to an adult, there is someone to go to. If the godparent can be seen as a trusted person for the godchild to confide in then this could be invaluable.

When Wendy's parents finally divorced after some years of misery, her godmother wrote her a letter explaining that there are often two sides to a story, that she shouldn't feel guilty about loving her wayward father. Her godmother also reminded her of her telephone number should she want to talk this week, this year, next year or whenever. Wendy has not often rung her godmother with specific parental problems, but she regularly emails about general "stuff".

When lives go wrong, adults can become very difficult, and they may become difficult with their children and also their friends. So keeping in touch with a godchild may also become difficult.

Sandy tried hard to maintain contact with his goddaughter after a close friend left his wife in acrimonious circumstances. Sadly, the goddaughter's mother would have nothing to do with any friend of her husband's and was prepared to sacrifice the godfather as a consequence.

It may be possible to persuade someone in these circumstances that it is not intended to take sides, but not always. If possible, but without being devious, open a direct and independent channel of communication with the child so that meetings do not depend upon the condition or goodwill of the parent. This is obviously easier if the child is older.

Sadly Jim doesn't speak with his mother any more. In fact he hasn't spoken with her in 12 years. Today, however, Jim still communicates with his godmother living in North America. Fortunately the godmother speaks to the mother so at least she gets some news of her estranged firstborn.

Taking parental alcoholism as an example, broaching the subject of the difficulty with the child requires a great deal of tact, and not a little courage on the part of the godparent. It may be easiest to talk about it by relating the similar circumstances of somebody else – therefore making it less personalised. Discussing such issues if possible is important. If a child does have an alcoholic parent, families themselves will rarely discuss the situation: it becomes the "elephant in the sitting room" and child ends up assuming that alcoholism is normal; that when the parent becomes randomly angry it is the child's fault; that the other parent is uncommunicative because they are boring when in fact they are scared. The child may start to blame themselves or blame both the alcoholic parent and the other parent for the problem but hate themselves for doing so. An outsider who gently puts other perspectives (such as mental health, work problems) on the problem and helps to explain to the child that they are not to blame will make a significant difference. In extremis, it may be worth trying to find out if the child's school is aware of problems, and see if the other parent can be persuaded to appraise the school of events.

Penny invited her gauche and difficult teenage goddaughter Dawn to lunch ostensibly to discuss hair colour. Rose was keen that Dawn had nice highlights put in her hair – Dawn had every intention of chopping it all off and dyeing it black.

"You know ill-health and early retirement can be a terrible thing for an ambitious man." "??" "When I first knew them your parents were such fun, so exciting, so sexy." "???" "There was real chemistry there". Dawn chopped off her hair anyway, dyed it black, and alienated the boys, but at least from those few words she understood her father's alcoholism much better and was comforted in knowing that there had been a point to her parents' marriage.

If a family member of a godchild develops terminal illness, it is helpful to find out as much as possible as to the nature of the disease and its likely progression and prognosis. The patient may or may not want to discuss it – one would hope that they will discuss it as it may well be helpful for them and the family, but people cannot be forced to discuss such matters if they don't want to.

If the mother of the godchild develops malignant melanoma, and feels unable to discuss the prognosis, an informed doctor probably give some clue as to what might lie ahead, and at least the ranges of possibility. The godparent might research childhood bereavement, as the bereavement process will start sooner than the day the parent dies. Behaviour may well be affected, and understanding the signals of distress will be helpful.

In cases where childhood or adolescence is disrupted, and connections lost, the godparent often serves a very useful role as a "vessel of information".

Lizzie's godmother performed precisely this role when her mother died after a protracted period of illness in her teens. Her godmother was able to tell her much of her mother's earlier life, her early marriage, and help find others who had been connected to her mother but got lost somewhere along the way. At that time Lizzie and her sisters were just legally old enough to live alone and look after themselves. Again the godmother stepped in regularly to help with "A" Level studies and to ensure they had a reason to get out of bed in the morning. Lizzie went on to university - she would never have got the necessary grade if her godmother hadn't been around to coax her into making the effort. Much later, after her father died and Lizzie had to pack up his flat, her godmother helped to deal with tedious letters from insurance companies, or clinics reminding the deceased to attend check-ups, something Lizzie really could not face at the time.

With regard to family dynamics, a godparent can be very useful in being outside the chain of discipline. The godparent need not condone behaviour, but may be of value as a steam outlet on a pressure cooker. Parents can expect a lot from their children, and "trouble" may be more perceived than real. Some parents, from an early age, worry about their children's behaviour when in fact the behaviour can be fairly normal. In these instances, a godparent may be able to calm things down or add a sense of humour / perspective. A godparent could also have a child to stay for a cooling off period.

The real trouble spots are likely to materialise during adolescence. Problems often revolve around smoking, drink, drugs, sex and sexuality, eating and anti-social behaviour. If a teenager comes to discuss any of these issues with the godparent , then they are probably asking for help or advice. If one observes behaviour in any of these areas, but the godchild has not come forward to discuss it, then it is more difficult to intervene. Young people's attitudes to risk are very different to older people's, which is why it is so difficult to persuade them not to adopt risky behaviours, even though they may be in possession of the facts. It is always worth bearing in mind that while the current behaviour may be worrying, it may change in the course of time.

The plethora of crises that could arise range from taking drugs, abuse of alcohol, being expelled from school, sexuality, pregnancy to name but a few. In summary the godparent's approach should be a combination of:

- Supporting the godchild,
- Support the parents,
- Accepting the godchild but possibly not the behaviour. The godparent doesn't have to abandon their own moral principles but if they express their own position they can hopefully continue to accept the godchild,
- Not betray confidentiality and probably only speak with the parents about the issue after obtaining permission from the godchild,
- Visit appropriate webb sites, talk with specialists to deepen understanding on situations eg illnesses, cancer, drug abuse, etc. and
- Pray like mad.

Beth, who went to a very sophisticated school, simply assumed that sex at thirteen was normal and was setting about how to dispose of her virginity. Fortunately, her much older sister picked up on this activity and immediately took her to one side. Once it had been suggested that university might be a better moment to pick her "debut", the thirteen-year-old accepted it without question and waited until the age of nineteen. It didn't matter that the advice came from her sister, and if her parents had raised it - sex was never discussed - she would have probably gone along with their advice. It was simply that the only behavioural option had been suggested by her peers and she had no means of comparison. So a godparent could have been useful.

Chapter 10

FROM A GUILT TO A GRATITUDE

Parents bringing up children are in a position to tell of the rewards and tribulations. They have little choice in the level of involvement they have as most of the responsibility for the upbringing falls on them.

Godparents have been asked to share this responsibility and most accept willingly. If they can do so in a way that meets the realistic expectations of both parties then sharing the role of godparenting should be more of a pleasure than a chore.

If this book has in some way stimulated a better understanding of what the role can involve and how rich the resulting relationship can be then hopefully fewer godparents will feel guilty and more will feel grateful that they were chosen to be a godparent and play such a valuable role in the upbringing of a child.

Godfather Graham used to remind his godchildren of one of the most important thing he had learnt in life - live simply, give generously and celebrate often

Appendix 1 Alternative Church Ceremony

Thanksgiving for the birth of a child

Minister
We have come here today to mark the birth of _____and celebrate with you his parents, the family members, godparents and friends the safe arrival of this child.

Minister
God who made the earth and everything beautiful in it
We thank you for all the good things in this world
For the gift of children
For the gift of ______
We thank you for a safe delivery
For the health of the mother
For the privilege of parenthood
And for the joy we can share
Accept our thanks we pray
Amen

Reading
A poem
A psalm e.g. Psalm 23, 100
A reading e.g. Mark 10 v13-16 Jesus & children
Luke 1 v46-55 Mary's song
1 Sam 2 v1-10 Hannah's song
Parents and godparents may want to say what they hope for in the life of the child

Minister
Godparenting is an ancient custom practiced in many cultures and in many countries across the world
The unique relationship that can develop between godchild and godparents can be a source of mutual joy and reward. In a world of change this relationship can provide a point of stability and guidance.
Together with the parents you are embarking on a new life giving adventure!

Promises
Who are the parents and godparents of _______?
We are.
Do you promise to help _______ realize his / her potential?
We will
Will you try and contribute towards his / her personal development as he / she grows up?
We will
Will you encourage her as he / she grows physically, spiritually and emotionally?
We will
Will you seek to be a guide and a safe haven in the years to come?
We will.

Minister
God who gives abundantly
Look in favour on this child
Grant that being nourished with all goodness he / she may grow and realize his / her full potential
May his / her parents and godparents have all the wisdom, patience and perseverance needed
May his / her life with the support given and your help make this world more just, more loving and more as you intended
Amen

Poem / reading

May God bless you and watch over you
May God make his face to shine upon you and be gracious to you
May God look kindly on you and this child and give you many days of happiness together and give you his grace.

Amen

Appendix 2 Proposed Secular Ceremony

Naming ceremony / thanksgiving

Leader (could be parents/ godparents / sponsors / grandparents)

On [date] [name of child] was born. Today we would like to celebrate with you the safe arrival of this child

Parents and godparents may want to say what they hope for in the life of the child

To bring [name] up to realize his/her potential we will need the support of you our family and friends. The parents and godparents have a special role to play in this child's growth.

Leader
Godparenting is an ancient custom practiced in many cultures and in many countries across the world
The unique relationship that can develop between godchild and godparents can be a source of mutual joy and reward. In a world of change this relationship can provide a point of stability and guidance.
Together with the parents you are embarking on a new life giving adventure!

Promises
Who are the parents and sponsor / godparents of ________?
We are.
Do you promise to be help ________ realize his / her potential?
We will
Will you try and contribute towards his / her personal development as he / she grows up?
We will
Will you encourage her as he / she grows physically, spiritually and emotionally?
We will
Will you seek to be a guide and a safe haven in the years to

come?
We will.

In closing here are some proverbs/poetry to provide food for thought as we celebrate the arrival of [name] and look forward to the years to come:

Proverbs
"Let another man praise you, and not you yourself, a stranger and not your own lips."
"A good name is rather to be chosen than great riches."
"Let not mercy and truth forsake thee, bind them about your neck. Write them upon the tablet of your heart."

Dryden
A thing of beauty is a joy for ever: its loveliness increases:
It will never pass into nothingness, but still will keep a bower
Quiet for us, and a sleep full of sweet dreams, and health and quiet breathing.

Sheenagh Pugh - Sometimes
Sometimes things don't go, after all,
from bad to worse. Some years, muscadel
faces down frost; green thrives, the crops don't fail,
Sometimes a man aims high, and all goes well.

A people sometimes will step back from war;
Elect an honest man; decide they care
Enough that they can't leave some stranger poor.
Some men become what they were born for.

Sometimes our best efforts do not go
Amiss; sometimes we do as we meant to.
The sun will sometimes melt a field of sorrow
That seemed hard frozen: may it happen for you.

Bibliography

F Bridger	Children Finding Faith
G Legood & I Markham	The Godparent's Handbook
M Withers	The Gifts of Baptism
E Bookser Barkley	When you are a godparent
T Sheridan	The gift of godparents
E Ramshaw	The Godparent Book
P Garrison	A Guide for Godparents

Lightning Source UK Ltd.
Milton Keynes UK
UKOW06f1916221215

265277UK00008B/215/P

9 781845 490768